by Rebecca Phillips-Bartlett

Minneapolis, Minnesota

Credits

Images are courtesy of Shutterstock.com. With thanks to Getty Images, Thinkstock Photo, and iStockphoto. Recurring images – gravity_point, inspiring.team, Gaidamashchuk, Zakharchenko Anna. Cover – Inspiring, adecvatman, BAZA Production, elenabsl, graphixmania, MaryDesy. 3 – yusufdemirci, GoodStudio. 4–5 – Monkey Business Images, New Africa, TinnaPong, Africa Studio, Walnut Bird, Marcelo Ricardo Daros, Tartila, adecvatman. 6–7 – Friends Stock, LightField Studios, Anatolir, Danielala, yusufdemirci, Monkey Business Images, AnnGaysorn. 8–9 – Drazen Zigic, Monkey Business Images, LightField Studios, Fagreia, yusufdemirci, Max kegfire. 10–11 – Dreams Come True, maitree summat, Janis Abolins, Maji Design, MOHAMMAD AZIZUL AMIRUL, Sudowoodo, Frau aus UA, TinnaPong, Iconic Bestiary. 12–13 – Halfpoint, A.RICARDO, ChipVector, top dog, 24K-Production, Marco Ciccolella, FocusDzign, ClassicVector, yusufdemirci, liluydesign. 14–15 – PeopleImages.com - Yuri A, matimix, Colorfuel Studio, GoodStudio, Krafted, Cassiohabib, fizkes. 16–17 – Ground Picture, Odua Images, AnnaKoles, adecvatman, PeopleImages.com - Yuri A, Jasen Wright, small smiles, Walnut Bird. 18–19 – John Kasawa, gvictoria, CapturePB, Sergey Novikov, yusufdemirci, Gorynvd, Bahau, Denis Maliugin, MNStudio. 20–21 – Drazen Zigic, matimix, ONYXprj, GoodStudio, Fagreia, Kzenon, Martial Red. 22–23 – FAMILY STOCK, Alla_vector, Fagreia, Jihan Nafiaa Zahri, BRG.photography, svtdesign, Tribalium. 24–25 – matimix, plo, smikeymikey1, Image Source Collection, Tribalium, Martial Red. 26–27 – Lopolo, Chanintorn.v, adecvatman, Robert Kneschke, Alexander_Safonov, svtdesign, yusufdemirci. 28–29 – Rawpixel.com, LeManna, Sergey Novikov, Ground Picture, Simply Amazing, Pretty Vectors. 30 – Alena Ozerova, BearFotos, Blan-k, Anatolir.

Library of Congress Cataloging-in-Publication Data is available at www.loc.gov or upon request from the publisher.

ISBN: 979-8-88916-460-9 (hardcover)
ISBN: 979-8-88916-465-4 (paperback)
ISBN: 979-8-88916-469-2 (ebook)

For more information, write to Bearport Publishing, 5357 Penn Avenue South, Minneapolis, MN 55419.

CONTENTS

WHAT IS A LIFESTYLE?

Your **lifestyle** is the way that you live your life. The things you do each day, from the foods you eat to your favorite activities, are all a part of your lifestyle.

WHAT IS YOUR FAVORITE ACTIVITY? DO YOU PLAY A SPORT OR HAVE ANY HOBBIES?

A HEALTHY LIFESTYLE

A healthy lifestyle means doing things to keep your mind and body healthy. That might include eating well and moving your body every day. Getting plenty of sleep is another important part of a healthy lifestyle.

A HEALTHY LIFESTYLE CAN HELP YOU FEEL HAPPIER AND STRONGER.

A HEALTHY MIND

Taking care of your mind is another important part of a healthy lifestyle. Having healthy **relationships**, taking time to relax, and doing things you enjoy are great ways to keep your mind healthy.

MAKING HEALTHY CHOICES

Your lifestyle is made up of many choices. Do you keep active? What kind of foods do you eat? And what do you do to make yourself happy? You don't need to make the perfect choice every time to have a healthy lifestyle. However, it is important to understand how different choices might make you feel.

MAKING SOME HEALTHY CHOICES MIGHT SEEM DIFFICULT AT FIRST. BUT WITH PRACTICE, THEY CAN BECOME AS EASY AS BRUSHING YOUR TEETH.

WHAT IS FITNESS?

Fitness means keeping your body strong and healthy with exercise. Keeping fit makes it easier to do everyday activities without getting tired.

WHY DO I NEED EXERCISE?

Exercise keeps your heart, muscles, and lungs healthy. It can also make you stronger and more **flexible**, which will make you less likely to get injured. **Physical** fitness can give you more **energy** and even improve your mood.

HOW MUCH EXERCISE?

Most young people should do at least one hour of exercise each day. Whether you play on a sports team or run around with your friends, there are plenty of ways to get your daily hour of exercise.

WHAT IS YOUR FAVORITE WAY TO EXERCISE?

You may not always have a full hour to exercise every day. Do what you can! Even 20 minutes of physical activity a day helps keep you fit.

TYPES OF EXERCISE

There are many kinds of exercises. Different types help different parts of your body. Doing a variety of exercises keeps your whole body in great shape.

AEROBIC

Aerobic exercises make your heart beat faster than usual. This keeps your heart strong and healthy. Most of the exercise that you do each week should be aerobic. Try running, biking, swimming, or dancing.

SPORTS WITH LOTS OF RUNNING, SUCH AS FOOTBALL AND BASKETBALL, ARE GOOD AEROBIC EXERCISES.

MUSCLE-STRENGTHENING

Every time you move your body, your muscles are put to work. Muscle-strengthening exercises make your muscles work harder than normal. This helps them get stronger. You should do these kinds of exercises about three times a week. You could play tug of war, go rock climbing, or do some push-ups.

FREEZE! EVEN WHEN YOU HOLD YOUR BODY COMPLETELY STILL, YOU ARE USING YOUR MUSCLES.

BONE-STRENGTHENING

Bone-strengthening exercises put **pressure** on your bones, which helps them get stronger. You should do these activities at least three times a week. Lots of these exercises, including running, skipping, or playing tennis, are also aerobic exercises.

Levels of Exercise

Sometimes, exercises feel easy to do, and other times they feel very hard. These differences are called levels of **intensity.** The intensity of an exercise is based on how hard it makes your body work.

An Intensity Scale

We can think of exercise intensity on a scale from 0 to 10. At 0, there is no effort, and 10 is our maximum possible effort.

0 is sitting and resting.

5-6 may be walking quickly or biking slowly.

7+ could be jogging, hiking uphill, or biking quickly.

10 is an all-out run.

YOU SHOULD DO EXERCISES THAT ARE IN THE MIDDLE AND UPPER INTENSITY EACH WEEK.

Different people have different levels of fitness. This means that the same exercise might feel easy for one person but difficult for someone else.

THE TALK TEST

The talk test is one way to figure out how intense an activity is for you. If you can talk while doing an exercise, but you are not able to sing, then it is a middle, or moderate, intensity exercise. When doing a high-intensity exercise, you will be able to say only a few words before needing to take a breath.

Finding your Sport

One of the most popular ways to exercise is by playing sports. Whether you prefer competing on a team or alone, there is a sport for everyone.

TRYING NEW SPORTS CAN HELP YOU MAKE NEW FRIENDS AND DISCOVER SOMETHING YOU ENJOY. THIS WILL KEEP YOUR MIND AND BODY HEALTHY.

TEAM SPORTS

Team sports are a great way to exercise while having fun with friends. Often, each player has a different role within a team. Whether you prefer running a lot, scoring points, or defending a goal, there is a job for you!

WHICH SPORTS COULD YOU JOIN AT SCHOOL?

SOLO SPORTS

Do you prefer exercising by yourself? There are plenty of sports to choose from. Swimming, biking, and running are great solo sports. Doing these alone lets you set your own goals.

YOU CAN DO MANY SOLO SPORTS WITH A FRIEND WHEN YOU WANT!

SECRET SPORTS

There are also a lot of ways to stay fit that don't involve typical sports. Why not plan a treasure hunt with your friends and then race one another to find the clues? Maybe you enjoy dancing around your home to your favorite tunes!

SPORTS FOR ALL

Exercise is for everyone! But some sports can be harder for people with **disabilities**. Fortunately, lots of sports have adapted to be **accessible** to **athletes** of all abilities.

WHAT IS YOUR FAVORITE WAY TO MOVE?

THE PARALYMPICS

The Paralympic Games is a sporting event for disabled athletes held every four years. Athletes **compete** against others with similar disabilities. Many different sports are part of the Paralympics, including cycling, swimming, hockey, and rugby.

SUPER SPORTS!

WHEELCHAIR BASKETBALL

Wheelchair basketball is a team game played entirely in wheelchairs. It was invented more than 75 years ago.

BOCCIA

Boccia is a ball game that was first played by people with cerebral palsy. This disability makes moving and speaking difficult.

GOALBALL

Goalball is a team game that uses a ball with bells inside. This allows people who are **blind** and partially sighted to hear where the ball moves.

FUEL FOR FITNESS

Everything you do, from running hard to sitting quietly, uses energy. All this energy needs fuel. The food you eat is broken down and turned into energy inside your body. Eat the right food so your body has the right fuel.

THE KINDS OF FOODS YOU USUALLY EAT MAKE UP YOUR DIET.

A BALANCED DIET

Having a balanced diet is the best way to make sure your body is getting the energy it needs. A balanced diet means eating different types of foods in the amounts that are right for you.

EATING FOR ENERGY

Before you exercise, make sure you give your body plenty of fuel. Carbohydrates give your body a lot of its energy. Foods that release carbohydrates slowly, such as whole grain crackers or granola bars, are good to eat one to three hours before exercising.

FRUIT, SUCH AS BANANAS AND APPLES, IS A GREAT SNACK TO EAT JUST BEFORE YOU EXERCISE.

WATER

Water is good for you, too! When you exercise, your body loses more water than usual. It is important to drink plenty of water before, during, and after you exercise.

Staying Safe

Exercise helps your body stay healthy. But sometimes, working your body too hard can lead to injuries. Fortunately, there are plenty of things that you can do to stay safe.

FOOTBALL HELMET

PROTECTIVE EQUIPMENT

For some sports, you need to wear protective clothing, such as knee pads, mouthguards, or helmets. Before you start playing, make sure you have the equipment you need to stay safe.

HOCKEY HELMET

DIFFERENT SPORTS NEED DIFFERENT TYPES OF HELMETS.

KNOW YOUR GAME

Some sports have lots of rules designed to keep everybody safe. Make sure you know these rules and always listen to coaches and referees.

PADS PROTECT YOU IF YOU FALL OR GET KNOCKED DOWN.

LISTEN TO YOUR BODY

While you exercise, be sure to listen to your body so you don't push yourself too far. If you exercise when you're sick or injured, you're more likely to hurt yourself. Look out for other athletes, too. Tell an adult if another player seems unwell, and let friends know if their shoelaces are untied.

WARMING UP

It is important to warm up your body before exercising. This gets it ready for activity. Warming up can help you perform better. It can also keep you from getting hurt.

HOW TO WARM UP

A warm-up should start with light aerobic exercise, such as gentle jogging. This will get your heart beating faster.

Next, you should gently stretch your muscles. Try to do active stretches, which keep you moving during the stretch.

Finally, a warm-up can have **drills** for your specific kind of exercise. Drills may include dribbling or passing the ball. Doing drills can help you react more quickly during a game.

COOLING DOWN

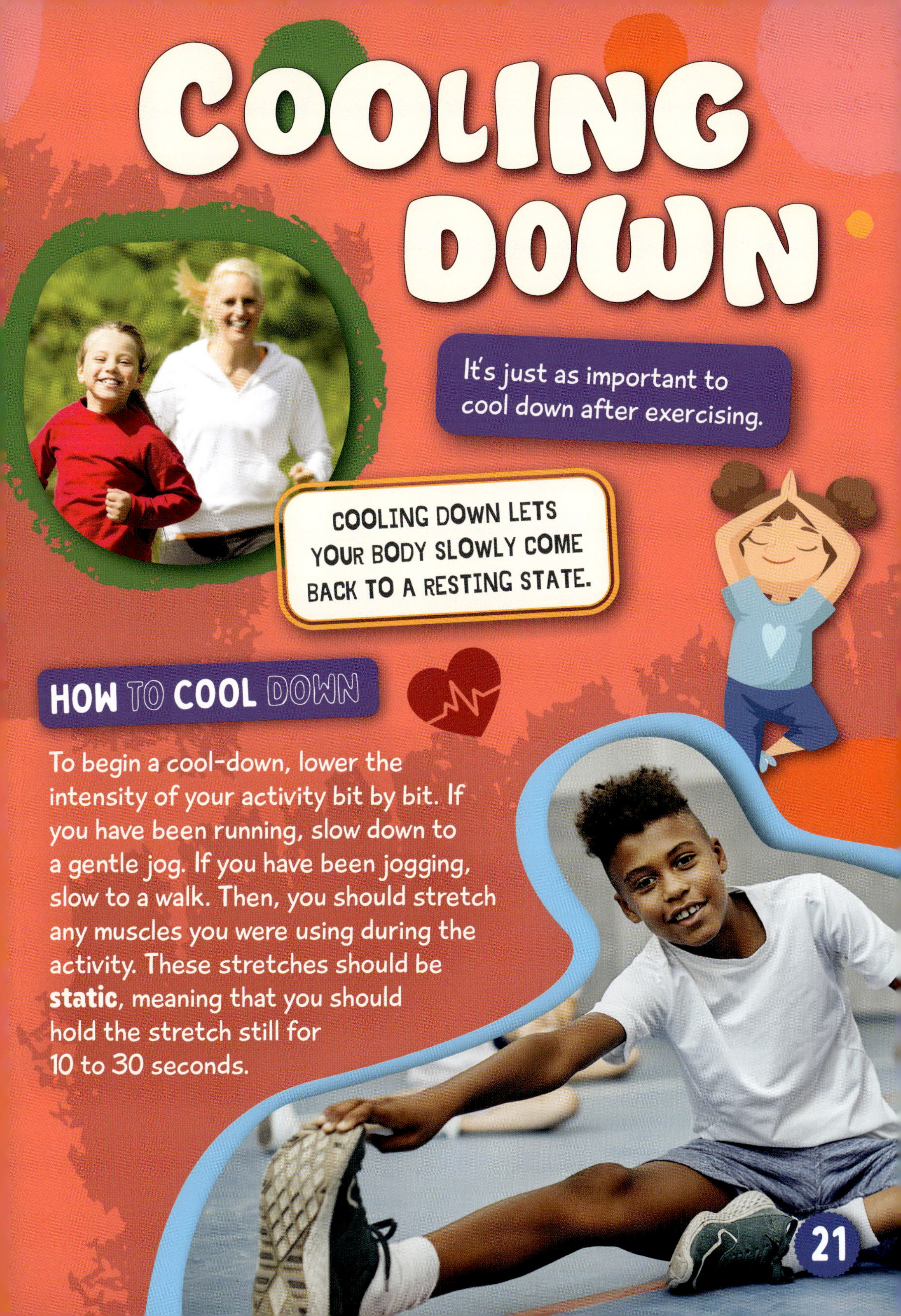

It's just as important to cool down after exercising.

COOLING DOWN LETS YOUR BODY SLOWLY COME BACK TO A RESTING STATE.

HOW TO COOL DOWN

To begin a cool-down, lower the intensity of your activity bit by bit. If you have been running, slow down to a gentle jog. If you have been jogging, slow to a walk. Then, you should stretch any muscles you were using during the activity. These stretches should be **static**, meaning that you should hold the stretch still for 10 to 30 seconds.

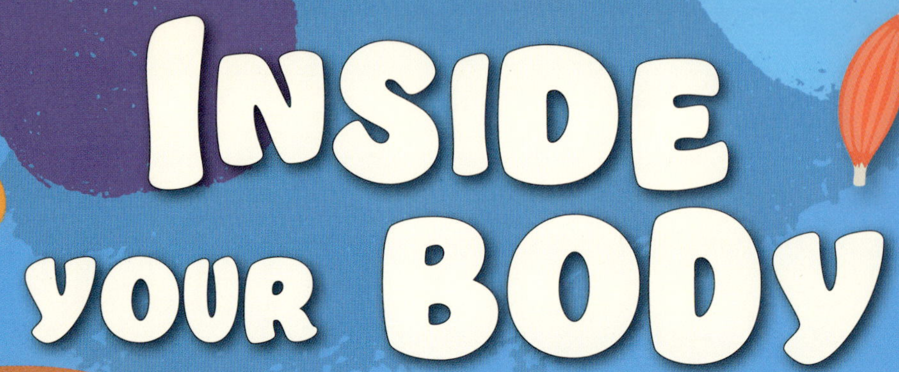

INSIDE YOUR BODY

Exercising makes your body work harder than usual. To keep up with this extra work, lots of things happen inside your body.

WHEN YOU EXERCISE, DO YOU FEEL **HOT** OR **OUT OF BREATH?**

THE LUNGS AND HEART

Your body needs **oxygen** to work. When you breathe, your lungs take in oxygen, which then goes into your blood. Your heart pumps the blood around your body. When you exercise, your heart beats faster than usual so your muscles can get all the oxygen they need.

MUSCLES

Your body has more than 600 muscles. They work hard every time you exercise. This hard work makes your muscles stronger. Some exercises might start to feel easier the more you do them.

YOUR HEART IS A MUSCLE! EXERCISE CAN MAKE IT STRONGER.

FEELINGS

Exercise can even change your mood! When you exercise, your body releases several kinds of brain chemicals. These chemicals can make you feel more relaxed, happier, and less worried.

YOUR BODY IN ACTION

When you exercise, you start to breathe faster. Depending on how intense your exercise is, you might notice a few other things, too.

YOUR HEART BEATS AROUND 100,000 TIMES EACH DAY!

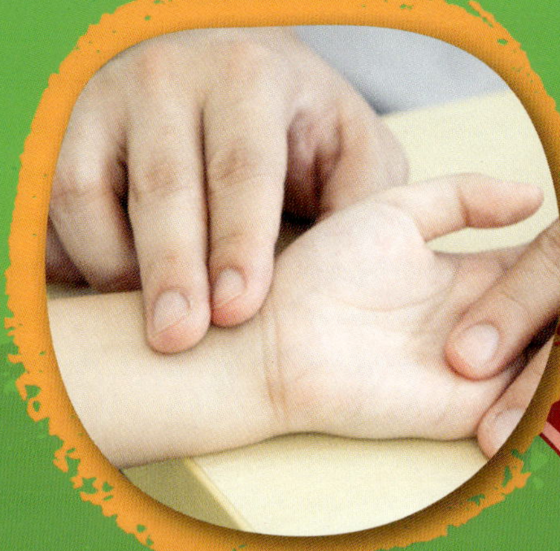

PULSE

Checking your pulse is one way of finding out how fast your heart is beating. Lightly press two fingers on your wrist below the thumb. When you find the right spot, you will feel a beat. Count the number of beats in a minute. This will tell you your heart rate.

GOING RED

During exercise, you may notice that your face and body start to turn red. This is because the blood moving around your body comes closer to the surface of your skin when you exercise. It does this to release heat, but it makes you look red, too.

YOUR FACE MIGHT ALSO TURN RED IF YOU FEEL EMBARRASSED.

SWEAT

Sweat is another way your body tries to cool itself down. Sweat is water released on the skin. As it evaporates, it takes heat energy from your body. This helps to keep your body at a comfortable temperature.

WHEN YOU SWEAT, YOU NEED TO DRINK PLENTY OF WATER TO AVOID GETTING **DEHYDRATED**.

AFTER EXERCISE

Once we're done exercising, we still need to take care of our bodies. This can be a big part of staying healthy.

TAKING A BREAK

It is important to listen to your body to know when it needs to rest. It is normal for some muscles to ache slightly after intense exercise. However, if your muscles are very sore it might be time to give them a break. If you are sick or in pain, you definitely should rest so your body has time to recover.

PLAYING WITH FRIENDS CAN FEEL LESS TIRING THAN GOING FOR A HARD RUN.

INTENSITY

It's healthy to exercise every day. However, if you do high-intensity exercise one day, you might feel better doing a lower-intensity activity the next day. Having this balance will keep you healthy.

SLEEP

YOUNG PEOPLE NEED AROUND 9 TO 12 HOURS OF SLEEP EACH DAY.

Getting plenty of sleep is an important part of staying healthy. Sleep gives your body and brain a chance to recharge. This will help make sure you have plenty of energy and make it easier to focus.

MADE TO MOVE

Technology is great! It can make our lives easier and give us access to a ton of information. While technology can help us, we still have to be sure to stay active.

DON'T STAY STILL

Cars let us get places quickly. But for short trips, consider walking or riding your bike. It's fun to sit at a computer, but plan times to get outside to keep your body moving.

BORN TO COMPETE

Long ago, people had to stay active to find food to eat. These ancient hunters had to compete with others to find the best food. Today, a little bit of competition can be good for you. Joining a team sport or setting your own goals can encourage you to be your best.

MAKING CHOICES

Living well is all about making healthy choices. Try planning your activities to make sure you are allowing enough time for friends, fitness, and rest.

LOVE TO MOVE

Getting plenty of exercise is a lot easier when you choose exercises that you enjoy. Whether you want to try a competitive sports team or prefer playing with your friends, keep moving to live well!

ARE YOU EXCITED TO EXERCISE?

GLOSSARY

accessible designed to accommodate different peoples' needs

athletes people who do sports or other types of physical exercise

blind unable to see

compete to do a sport or activity, often with the goal of winning or doing better than others

dehydrated not having enough water in the body to be healthy

disabilities conditions that can limit someone's ability to do certain things

drills repetitive exercises to practice certain skills

energy the power used to do something

flexible able to bend easily

intensity how difficult something is

lifestyle a way of living that reflects the things a person finds important

oxygen a natural gas that living things need to survive

physical relating to the body

pressure a pressing force put on something

relationships the connections that people have with one another

static not moving

INDEX

READ MORE

Audra, Janari. *Physical Health in our World (Spotlight on our Future).* New York: PowerKids Press, 2022.

Loh-Hagan, Virginia. *Sports and Fitness (In the Know: Influencers and Trends).* Ann Arbor, MI: Cherry Lake Publishing, 2021.

LEARN MORE ONLINE

1. Go to **www.factsurfer.com** or scan the QR code below.
2. Enter "**Healthy Exercise**" into the search box.
3. Click on the cover of this book to see a list of websites.